C000148590

How to Make a Woman Out of Water

Charles Bennett

How to Make a Woman
Out of Water

ENITHARMON PRESS

First published in 2007
by Enitharmon Press
26B Caversham Road
London NW5 2DU

www.enitharmon.co.uk

Distributed in the UK by
Central Books
99 Wallis Road
London E9 5LN

Distributed in the USA and Canada
by Dufour Editions Inc.
PO Box 7, Chester Springs
PA 19425, USA

© Charles Bennett 2007

ISBN: 978-1-904634-42-3

Enitharmon Press gratefully acknowledges the financial support of
Arts Council England, London.

British Library Cataloguing-in-Publication Data.
A catalogue record for this book is available
from the British Library.

Designed by Libanus Press
and printed in England by
Antony Rowe Ltd

I hear the rain outside
To help me to go to sleep

W S GRAHAM

ACKNOWLEDGEMENTS

Thanks are due to the editors of the following publications where these poems, sometimes in earlier versions, first appeared: *Daps, Envoi, Iota, New Welsh Review, Ploughshares, Poetry London, Poetry Wales, Rain Dog, Raw Edge, The Rialto, The Shop, Stand, Staple, The Times Literary Supplement.*

'The Drowned Radio' is included in *Radio Waves* (Enitharmon Press, 2004), edited by Seán Street, and 'How to Make a Woman Out of Water' was short-listed for the Strokestown International Poetry Competition 2002.

'Bat' is a companion poem to Mark Doty's 'Pipistrelle'. We saw the same bat one evening and, unknown to each other at the time, wrote about it the next morning. The poems appear together in *Ploughshares*, Vol. 31, No. 4 (Winter 2005–06). Mark kindly includes me in his poem – I apologise for not returning the favour, and acknowledge his generosity here.

Thanks are also due to all the wise readers who helped these poems find themselves, especially Gillian Clarke and, of course, my wonderful doctor, to whom this book is dedicated.

CONTENTS

RAIN

Late or early or else
gone to the wrong address
I am a god most
in need of forgiveness.

I love the way you
wonder if I'm near
by holding out the flat
of your hand in prayer.

Weeds and roses alike
sip at every drop –
they know I only fall to
lift them up.

Tonight I pour
entirely for your sake
and call my name harder and
harder on the lake.

HALF MOON BAY

Nights I couldn't sleep in California
I remembered the alders back home
and left those damp, deciduous thoughts
in pillows wherever I went –

a trail you may well discover
if ever you stop for the night
in Half Moon Bay.

Lying in the dark you'll find
you're thinking of a deep-rooted species
partial to rivers and streams –

and falling asleep you'll notice
how a breeze through yellow leaves
sounds exactly like someone
taking a shower down the hall.

FAMILIAR TREES OF NORTH AMERICA

Under a Velvet Ash
she lets you make a wish.

In a glade of Water Birch
she trembles at your touch.

In a grove of Blue Oak
she does not need to speak.

In a stand of Quaking Aspen
she begins to cry for no reason.

In an orchard of Bitter Cherry
she is sorry.

In the shade of a Desert Willow
she says I told you so.

Beneath a Black Hawthorn
she leaves you alone.

A WOMAN MADE OF BEES

Alone in the cellar I remember how
she murmured across my desk –
a black velvet dress
stitched together with stings.

If I slipped my hand round her waist
I felt the darkness fizzing.
I could search all night and never find
the quiet, sweet queen.

I think of how she trembled
through my fingers, of how her music
ebbed through the keyhole drop by fuzzy drop.
With a cube of sugar on my tongue

in a room of empty jars
I remember the night I made her –
the slow delicious tickle
as I poured her over my face.

THE MAN IN THE WATERFALL

On the bus full of tourists I was happy –
the bump and slither of vodka
sang in Icelandic all the way
to where the waterfall waited,

the famous blue waterfall
of polished glacial ice
with its legend of a man inside.
Only a reflection said the driver

and only when light is friendly
only yourself you're glimpsing
in prisms of turquoise water
like a man frozen in tears.

But looking at the face I knew
it was time to release what I saw –
become the man in the waterfall
and watch the bus go back.

COMPREHENSION

If three men dig a hole three metres deep
and if three crows fly in to look for worms
and if three cats should follow them

(because they heard crow-music late at night)
and if it rains
and then the moon comes out –

How often does a crow dream of the moon?
How does the rain know when to stop?

How many leaves make an autumn?
How wet will it be by morning?

THE GOLDEN SOFA

Fast as I can and heavy
coming down I wallop the blunt
piano of carpetless stairs.

I'm dancing the blue shadow-bear
who likes to follow my sleeping
seven times seven to death.

The rooms are big with going
and only the golden sofa
will not leave. A deep lake

of syrup I must never lick,
in the room we saved for best
and did not use, I scrawl my name

in its plush with a sticky finger,
then run outside to watch my father
trickle our keys through the letterbox

like the note written in lemon juice
I've slipped between the floorboards
and left for the strangers to open.

GIFTED

When I found I could lift things up
simply by looking at them hard
and making it happen in my mind,

I'd wait till my parents were out
dance the wardrobe gently on the ceiling,
feel lighter myself at last.

I tickled a trawler over the harbour wall,
sent shoals of teaspoons hissing
down the street.

Now, when I look at cars
parked on the curb outside
I sip the pleasure of leaving

things exactly as they are.
As for these sycamore leaves
floated above my head –

tonight I'll touch them down
in our own personal autumn
of whispers and sighs.

THIS

This is the hot one I keep
   the same side always and this
is outside at Christmas with a key
   on string to open the present.

This is the red one going up
   to ask or answer and this
is a kite in the sky at summer
   on string with *down* at the end.

This is the green one over
   the hills and far and this
is a mole in his black who does not
   want to come out today.

This is the moon with his face
   on top of the dark and this
is the sea which sends the castle
   back to sleep.

This is the window with the man
   who looks when I see and this
is the bed where I close my eyes
   and open night.

This is a tree with leaves
   on the inside only and this
is the boy at the top of the tree
   never coming down anymore.

THE BOY IN THE PICTURE OF ATLANTIS

When the boy in the picture of Atlantis
on the cover of *Look and Learn*
calls me by name and waves

I see my mermaid girlfriend
whose body is an endless mystery
crying as I leave on the monorail –

she knows I can never return
to sing with our dolphin or kiss
in the sacred cave,

she knows I must sit and pretend
to be human and nothing more
in the back of this steamed-up Hillman Minx

waiting for my dry-land father
to flip the wipers awake
and look more clearly at the rain.

SEVEN SIXTEENTHS

There's a view of the ocean from my window
in this room above the garage where I live –
watercress sandwiches for lunch
a lawnmower open on the workbench
and the tang of Brasso to remind me
how the chrome on my father's Triumph Herald
has never been so clean.

Later, when I find the missing note
from the glockenspiel of spanners on the wall,
I'll hang it on the nail that's waiting for seven sixteenths.
But now there's time to repair
whatever seems to be wrong –
listening to the blackbird and the ocean
saying once again: this is heaven.

TWELVE ANGELS

The first removes your breath
and leaves what lies beneath.

The second brings a glance
of how you were happy, once.

Three takes away your skin
and you are no one then.

The gift of number four
is silence – nothing more.

Five goes off with your pulse
and gives you something else.

Six delivers a list
of every chance you lost.

Seven is gathering up
the moisture from your lip.

There's nothing eight likes better
than bringing an end to the matter.

When nine turns off your sight
you don't even give it a thought.

Ten brings terrible weather
to let you know it's over.

Eleven collects the sand
left at the back of your mind.

And twelve arrives with the dark
from which you will not walk.

THE ROOM

A sofa and two matching chairs
in the elbow of a country lane
have been abandoned so we
may rest for a while and say –
this is our living room.

NOTES ON THE ILLUSTRATIONS

Nymph entangled by sea snake with seven heads

The nymph's expression becomes
resonant with meaning once we learn
the serpent's seven heads
are portraits of distinguished philosophers.

This is an early work
from a period of relative contentment.
The colour of the monster's skin
derives from a pigment obtained

by crushing the seed pods of a tree
which grew in the artist's garden
and where he was often to be found
playing his guitar in its branches.

Man on bridge above river, seen from behind

Looking over his shoulder
we see the river emerging
from the roots of a stylised willow
in the top right-hand corner of the picture.

Two swans in the upper reaches
are possibly the artist and his wife
who was often to be encountered
working in the vegetable garden.

The approaching figure in a rowing boat
turning his face towards us
is the artist coming down river
to meet himself.

The old fisherman

The prow of the boat folds around him
suggesting we are seated in the stern
with a hand on the tiller
to steer the picture's meaning.

He is, you will notice, not fishing.
His pale impasto hands are loosely clasped.
Meanwhile, around us, as far
as the frame can see

all the fish he caught
and then released
are leaping in small rainbows
out of the lake.

FRIDAY ISLAND

There's a walk you can take on Friday Island
a walk in the steps of a botanist
who named four flowers in memory
of his daughter who drowned on Christmas Eve.

You'll find *Her Favourite Dress* for example
tilting yellow petals to the sun.

Her Voice in the Morning is pungent
when crushed between the fingers.

Asking for a Glass of Water
is attractive to the orange-tipped fritillary.

Hush Now and Go to Sleep
has leaves which taste of lemon.

At the end of the walk there's a grave
and the name of a brilliant man
who looked at the sea all day
and always dreamt of flowers.

THE BEACH

She sent him a stone from their beach
and kept on sending so often
in a room at the end of the landing
he'd never really known what to do with
he soon had a beach of his own.
He painted the walls that blue
which can either be sea or sky
and waited for seven days
after her stones had stopped –
it was all the time he needed
to hear the seagulls crying
to leave his cup on the drainer
fasten the door behind him
and seeing just then what he'd hoped for
slip into view round the headland,
swim towards her sail.

POPTY

All the bread on display
in this small bakery by the sea
is clarified and seasoned by a light
blown slant across wet tarmac in the car park.

Here is a cathedral made with loaves
a shrine of baps and oven-bottom cakes
of muffins, rolls and crumpets piled like prayers.

I grasp the back of a heavy stoneground loaf
and feel it sag with heat. But you must reach
past pitta, brioche and ciabatta
to land the floury flounder of a naan.

Tonight your vegetable Dhansak
sweet and hot and sour
will scald us into silence.

NANTUCKET

Your threadbare hooded sweatshirt
opens its arms on the line
to scare away disaster.

You waved from the lighthouse as if
the loveliest castaway ever
the day it came to hand.

Its washed-out red is a flag
guiding me in to harbour.
When I take it off the line it puts

one cool arm round my shoulder.
I fold it under your pillow
And know you'll be home tomorrow.

MWNT

1

You close your eyes as the tide
comes in and puts the beach
to sleep. It dreams of the sky
with a cloud in the shape of a kite.

I push my toes in sand. Nothing
we touch can be held for long –
that's what the twelve-spotted butterfish
tells our fingers. The ferry comes and goes

as if to say arriving and leaving behind
are one and the same. You've left me here
by going where you are, but don't wake up –

ignore the way those oyster-catchers
keep going off now and then
like alarm clocks with no sense of timing.

2

Falling asleep on the sand
is a kind of going out.
One by one the waves
open their slim white petals

and blossom along the shore.
The wail of a seagull turns
in your dream to the chime
of an ice-cream van.

There's nothing else to do
this afternoon, but wait until
the waves throw stones at us –

stones as thin as rain
that turn into worm pipefish
or narrow-leaved eelgrass.

3

Swimming in the sea while it rains
is a dream that tastes delicious.
A bee comes in to land
on the sheep-bit's prickled blue,

spaniels dash after driftwood.
Our gills have gone
the same way as our tails –
but you have found a way

to slip beneath the fresh
and take your sip of salt.
These waves do not disturb

and once this apricot stone
discovers the tree in itself
we'll sit in the shade together.

4

Is the memory of water
all that's left behind
when the tide goes out?
I watch the breaking waves

leave pieces of themselves
in tongues of snails who lick
away the rock. A skylark
sends your last known position

in a spill of continual Morse.
But who knows where you are –
your hair like bladder-wrack blossom

where swarms of common blenny
feed on the flowers by night
then hoard the bitter honey.

5

Jackdaws clatter and tumble down
the wind together. It's less like flying
more like being flung. You fall
asleep to throw yourself away

as far and deep as you can –
then spend the rest of the dark
chasing after yourself. When you
wake up we'll wait until two seals

appear in the bay. We'll see
how long it takes that skittish kite
to snag its string.

Collapsed in the car,
does it dream of being a blue
and yellow cloud?

6

Your eyelids flicker like two butterflies
rising on the updraft of each other.
When frost comes to sit on the bench
they'll drop like leaves that can't

remember their tree. A stone skips
over the water then dives in
as if there's nothing to fear from
going under. The waves repeat

a word which sounds like 'loss'
or else perhaps 'distress'.
Come back from where

you're neither down nor across
and tell me how you knew
all along it was 'kiss'.

7

Wasn't it you who told me how a bird
dreams of its song at night?
I'd like to think there's
music in the dark.

A trail of vapour chalks across the sky.
I think of letting a plumb-line down
until I touch the depth
of where you are.

Common starfish drift
in sticky constellations over rock.
When you wake up

will you tell me you dreamt
of rain? The tide goes out
as you come in again.

JACKDAW MORNING

Jackdaws on the chimney pots this morning.
You already gone.
Roses in the garden almost open.
Me rolling over onto your side.

Me almost gone with the jackdaws.
Your side over in the garden.
Morning rolling open on the chimney pots.
You already roses.

TWO SNAILS

Two snails mating on a stone
as I walk down to the sea
after a day of rain.

They loop and curl in a pool
of their own spittle. They clack
their mottled shells in slow applause.

Tomorrow I'll lick my finger
and spell the knot they make
on the small of your back.

I'll shape the slow strokes
in the deft, wet dance
of writing your name.

PILLOW MOTH

At night I fold my wings
into this soft oblong.
I make myself a haven
for her head.

I become the secret
lake she likes to
bathe in after dark –
one by smooth one

I taste her days.
I need to be crushed
with creases or else
I cannot grow afresh.

It takes all day to find
the long white silence
she listens to until
the night has flown.

SNOW HARE

Ears of drizzle and juniper
Snow sings you asleep above the moor.

Tongue of gorse and bilberry
Snow flecks you white behind the hill.

Nose of sedge and smoke
Snow is on your scent beside the loch.

Eyes of rowan and rain
Snow finds you blinking by the stream.

Feet of heather and storm
Snow sends you dancing over stone.

Coat of clouds and willow
Snow helps you hide in a hollow.

Hare of stars and frost
Snow makes you turn into a ghost.

BAT

Skittery between the beech trees
he follows the glance of his song.

His music makes us avoidable
as we wait for his scribble on our eyes.

What seems haphazard is only
the word *Listen!* turned into a life.

Thinking of what it means
to be true to music

by the edge of a wood in summer
as a question dances through the dark,

I call your name – and wait until
your answer sees me home.

LULLABY

Small dark mouth
in the smooth white bowl
halfway between
the hot tap and the cold

do not tell me
how the good I've made
blows away to nothing
like a cloud

do not let me
know that all my wrongs
sing tonight like birds with
bitter tongues

do not show me
every day I spend
falling through the mirror
till I'm blind

between the cool
and warm stay silent now
don't say another word
until tomorrow.

WINTER

words spoken in sleep
rise to the surface slowly

I lie in the dark and listen
while the orchard blossoms with frost

as if I were overhearing
a mermaid's cold song

notes of snow that leave
our bedroom white over

THE SLEEPWALKER

She's come outside to plant their forks and spoons.
She's dipped the stems in milk to help the fragile roots take hold.
She's left the knives behind because they have no flower heads.

She hopes that if they're in before the frost
She stands a chance of seeing them come into bloom.
She lets him pass them to her one by one.

He holds them by the neck between his thumb and index finger.
He knows she won't remember in the morning.
He watches her kiss each one goodbye and tell it to come home safe.

COME OUTSIDE NOW EVE

Come outside now Eve,
put on your little black dress –
I've found those pins your father
saved from his shirts,

the worn-out nibs of fountain pens
you did your home-work with,
a thorn of narwhal ivory
for sewing sailors' shrouds

and compass needles galvanised
with the sheen of a starling's wing
which point towards your door.
Lock it behind you Eve,

the key will be cold in your hand
when you come towards me barefoot
through the barbed-wire garden
wearing your dress of night.

THE SKIN

Once it was dead we ate every bit except
for the skin I admit it.

Which first we set alight except
nothing would ignite it.

Which second we thought to bury except
no hole was deep enough for it.

Which next we ripped with our knives except
their blades were splintered by it.

Which after we drowned far out at sea except
the tide returned it.

Which then we left for the rats except
they danced all night around it.

Which one of us hid from the rest except
all of us dreamt about it.

Which we kept quite safe in the end except
none of us knew where we'd put it.

Which one of us found in the woods except
he was in it –

THE SWIMMING POOL AT NIGHT

She likes to slip in late
alone after everyone else.

I explore the swirl of her ear
or hold her like an island as she floats.

And when she's gone, I send
the slow disturb of her through myself.

Making a tide from her touch
in the calm of dark.

SNOW

Me unbelievable clean over everything different

Into shapes you put me then like often

On all night not knowing when to stop

Square one next day you kiss and clutch me up

Me all over you all over me

Spattered patch where rabbits danced before

Stopping all the robins in their tracks

Then not really tasting me of anything much

The heavy of me everywhere unwanted

One in a car going home and never anymore

So otherwhere me again not saying bye in the dark

You unsorry back to normal glad

Then years gone after past your window now

You coming out to be in me

SISYPHUS

Halfway a hawthorn tree
is a talon which will not let go.
He severs nettles and brambles,
wraps them round his hands.

At first he used to curse
until his tongue turned black.
Now he sits to watch the river
signing its name through the field.

Each day he finds the nest,
the bush of bitter berries,
he strokes me to the summit by sunset.
How smooth I've grown beneath his hands!

He cools me with sweat when it's hot
and when it rains I feel
the fish of stone within me
start to swim.

THE BOY WHO WAS RAISED BY THE MEDUSA

I'd whistle to tell her I was home.
She'd whistle back to tell me where she was.

At night on my face her fingers
were drops of rain. Unwanted cats and dogs

left on our doorstep with a note
always made her sad. She liked

to watch the moon through a telescope,
sit in her shed in the orchard

smoking a pipe and singing. Her voice
put blossom on the branches.

Just look at that, she'd say.
I still have the set of sparrows

left by the bed for my birthday.
She made up her mind to keep me

and here I am. That's the mask she wore
when I read to her aloud every evening.

This is the full-length mirror
she was sprawling across when I found her.

THE SECRET OF THE SEVEN CIGARETTES

If we could only unravel
the furl of each cigarette
and read the name
printed in kohl letters
on wisps of paper

the secret of the seven cigarettes
smoked as the tide goes out
alone on a bench above town
just as it's growing dark
and a bird in a tree behind her
starts to sing

would all make perfect sense
and then perhaps we'd know
if this time she's giving up for good
as she puts them to her lips for a moment
until the name is only
seven blue sighs
blown at the sea.

FETCH

Now and again the woman
throwing a stick for her dog
down to where the waves are coming in

chuckles because he goes
chasing after a stick
she's only pretended to throw.

He dashes down the beach
barking at a stickless sky
his tail a kind of laughter

as he rushes back to her hand
bringing whatever she threw
instead of the stick.

SWIMMING OVER LONDON

A woman is swimming over London,
a fox turns up his face to see her pass.

There are blackbirds in the sleeping streets,
a pear tree luminous with blossom.

It's the dream she always has,
the dream where she's stretching out

until all the houses are gone
and the fields give way to a beach

where the yacht that's moored in the bay
has a light in its cabin window.

She smiles and swims over London,
darkness is a murmur in her hair.

A POSTCARD TO W S GRAHAM

Stopped at your house on way to Madron Well.
Knew you were out so went to shake hands
with cool smooth doorknob. Sorry
we couldn't take you and Nessie to Mousehole –
like to think of you eating a liquorice ice cream.

Way to well was muddy and overgrown.
Thought you might have been there now and again.
Knew you were gone so came to shake hands with water.
Rags were dripping in trees. All of them wishing
you were here and weather glorious.

THE DROWNED RADIO

Recovered by fishermen who saw
a chest of gold below them

its casing warped like ribs of carp
its needle stuck on Hilversum

this silted brain is working
perfectly still.

Stand by the water for a while
as a swan swims once round the island –

soon you'll become attuned
to the soft conversation of clouds

and notice how a minnow's heart
ticks with the drizzle of static.

HOW TO MAKE A WOMAN OUT OF WATER

Move to a boathouse by a river –
the walls must be yellow, the windowsills blue.
Sleep downstairs with your head upstream,
wait for a dream of swimming.

When it rains all night and you lie awake
collecting the music of a leak
and reading *The Observer's Book of Water*
until you've learned that chapter

on whirlpools and waterspouts by heart,
listen to her whisper and giggle
as she scribbles her slippery name
over and over down the glass.

Have a bucketful of oysters in the sink
in case she's feeling peckish
and a case of Rainwater sherry
chilling in a cave behind the waterfall.

At the bottom of the well
there's one white pebble –
put it beneath your tongue
until it dissolves into a kiss.

Become so dry she will slip
into the shape of your thirst.
Prepare to be a shiver on her surface.
Taste her arrival on the wind.

REVISION

My notebook, left by mistake
all night on the garden table
has been revised by rain –

blurs and dribbles swim
the lakes and shallow seas
of its brimming pages.

Put in the oven to dry,
drought begins to crinkle
the lip of every puddle –

and what comes out is a shell,
crisp and hollow and curled
round a fall of rain.